ARTIST TRANSCRIPTIONS

T0061517

CHICK COREA
Elektric Band II
PAINT THE WORLD

ISBN 978-1-4768-7422-7

HAL•LEONARD®
CORPORATION
7777 W. BLUEMOUND RD. P.O. BOX 13819 MILWAUKEE, WI 53213

CREDITS

If you would like to write to Chick, write:	CHICK COREA P.O. BOX 39581 Los Angeles, CA 90039
MANAGEMENT:	RON MOSS MANAGEMENT 2635 Griffith Park Blvd. Los Angeles, CA 90039
PERSONAL MANAGER:	Ron Moss
FRONT COVER CONCEPT:	Barton Stabler & Ron Moss
COVER ILLUSTRATION:	Barton Stabler
COVER DESIGN & LETTERING:	Mike Manoogian
MUSIC SCORE COMPILATION & EDITING:	Peter Sprague & Chick Corea
PHOTOS:	Harrison Funk

MY THANKS to Peter Sprague for his care in editing and transcribing.

And thanks to L. Ron Hubbard for his constant inspiration.

CONTENTS

PAINT THE WORLD

USE OF CHORD SYMBOLS
PHILOSOPHY

I use chord symbols as a direct invitation to the player to improvise and add his own notes and embellishments.

The chord symbols indicate the scale that I intend to go with the melody.

If the voicing of a chord is not written out note-for-note, it can be improvised by the player using the melody notes that are written and the chord symbol(s) guides.

I find it confusing to try to "write out" a voicing by only adding extra numbers and signs to the chord symbol itself. Usually the essential coloring notes are written as the melody line or as any other counter line that's written. In this case, all that's needed is the basic information about the harmony.

Chord symbols that indicate the first four notes in a chord (bottom to top) are usually sufficient to give all the information that the player needs, quickly and at-a-glance. (For example: C = C root, E third, G fifth, B seventh; G7 = G root, B third, D fifth, F seventh.)

I never include in the chord symbol altered notes that are in the written melody, (i.e. if there's a C♯ written in the melody and it's a G7 chord, I never add "♭5" to the symbol, as it's already written in the melody).

When there's an "important" note that the voicing needs, I first try to write the note into the part before attempting to add it as a number or a sign to the chord symbol.

Most "altered" notes are "passing tones" anyway — and if a little extra time is taken to write them into the music — often a nice counter melody begins to develop.

I use chord symbols for a quick appraisal of the basic harmony and scale of the part it applies to. They invite improvisation.

MEANING OF THE SYMBOLS

1) Triads and chords without 3rds or 7ths are called by just the letter of the root — i.e. C = C Major triad, E = E Major triad, etc.

2) The 7th degree of the chord is usually the highest number given in the symbol. The 9ths, 10ths, 11ths, etc. — aren't put in the chord symbol, as they're usually in the melody line.

3) The only times other notes in the chord are added after the basic root, 3rd & 7th (i.e. Dm7) is if the added notes are not in the melody line of that bar and are needed for the sound of the harmony. A♭9 or ♭5 is sometimes added.

4) The form of the chord symbol:

- Lower case "m" is used for "minor":
    Dm7, Cm

- Caps are used for all root notes:
    C7, F♯7

- "♭" and "♯" are used instead of "-" and "+":
    D♭7, B♭m♯5

- Other than the basic root, 3rd/7th construction, added notes are done in smaller size as above:
    Cm7♭5, C7♭9

- "△" is used for "Major 7th":
    C△ = "C Major 7th"

- "ø" or "m7♭5" are used for half diminished 7th chords:
    Dø7 or "Dm7♭5"

- Horizontal slash is used when a bass note, different than the root of the chord symbol, is needed:
    Dm7, C△, F7, etc.
    ‾G‾ E E♭
  chord on top; bass note on bottom.

- The chord symbols should be placed right above (or below — depending on staff construction) the melody note it starts on.

- Glossary:
  a) Dm7   D m   7
           (1) (2) (3)   see below
     (1) - root of chord
     (2) - 3rd
     (3) - type of 7th — when without "♯" — it means dominant 7th or ♭7
  b) m = minor
  c) △ = Major 7th
  d) ø = half diminished
  e) Dm7 = chord
     ‾G‾ = bass note
  f) C = C Major triad

Chick Corea

ElektricBand II

A FEW ADDED NOTES by Chick Corea

Paint The World	An attempt to use a "loop" with the underlying piano figure that recurs over and over again. Why not?
Blue Miles	Based on a phrase from a Miles Davis solo on the song "Straight No Chaser" by Monk from a live album including Cannonball Adderly, John Coltrane, Jimmy Cobb, Paul Chambers.
Tone Poem	Written especially for Elektric Band 2.
Space	Inspired by the track on Salif Keita's album "Soro;" especially the bass line which I transcribed and adapted.
The Ant & The Elephant	An attempt to use the "acoustic" piano sound along with the full sound of the electric guitar. (It's easier to do in a recording studio with separation and headphones than to do live.)
Tumba Island	Learned the "Tumba" – which is currently a popular dance in the Caribbean Islands – from a boy named Xemio Jacobs, whom I met in Bonaire playing with his father's band.
Ritual	An attempt at a rhythmic "crossfade" between 4/4 swing and funk.
Ished	Inspired by the Miles Davis bands of the early '70s.
Spanish Sketch	Inspired by the classic album "Sketches of Spain" by Miles Davis and Gil Evans.

PAINT THE WORLD

By CHICK COREA
and GARY NOVAK

BLUE MILES

By CHICK COREA

10

Fine

TONE POEM

By CHICK COREA

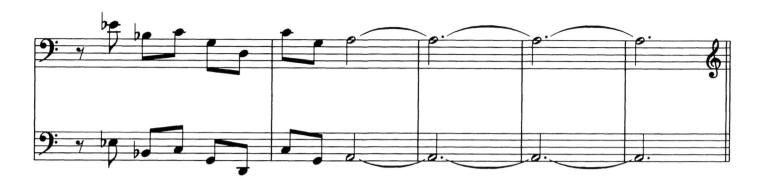

D solo changes

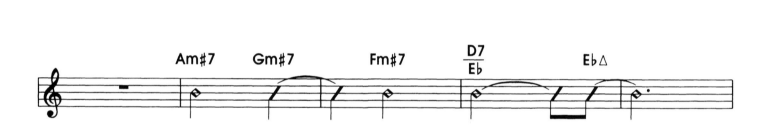

SPACE

By CHICK COREA
(bass line adapted from
SALIF KEITA's "Waraya")

back to A *for solos*
use B *as an interlude between solos*

THE ANT & THE ELEPHANT

By CHICK COREA

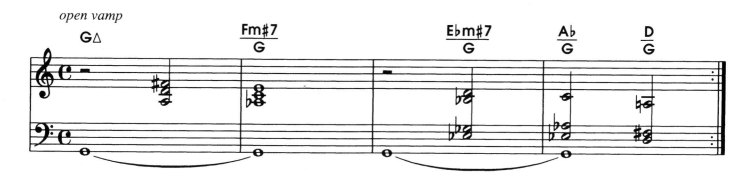

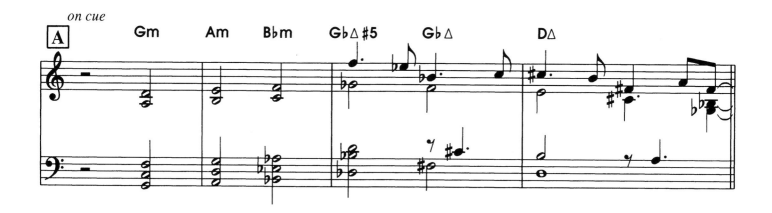

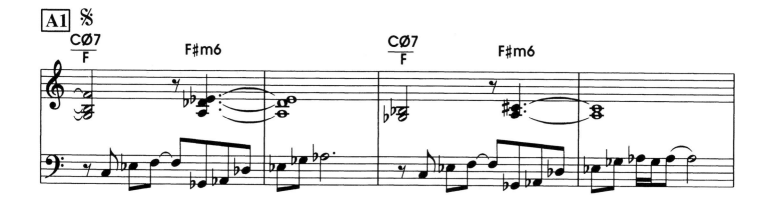

TUMBA ISLAND

By CHICK COREA

RITUAL

By CHICK COREA

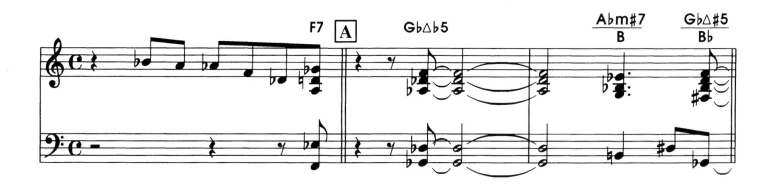

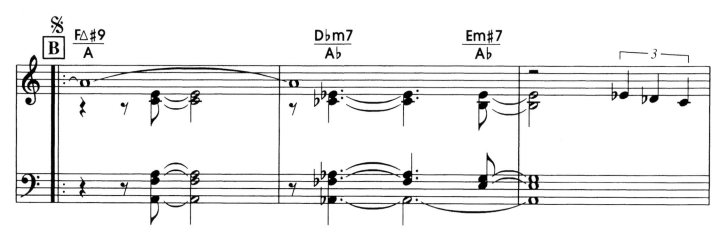

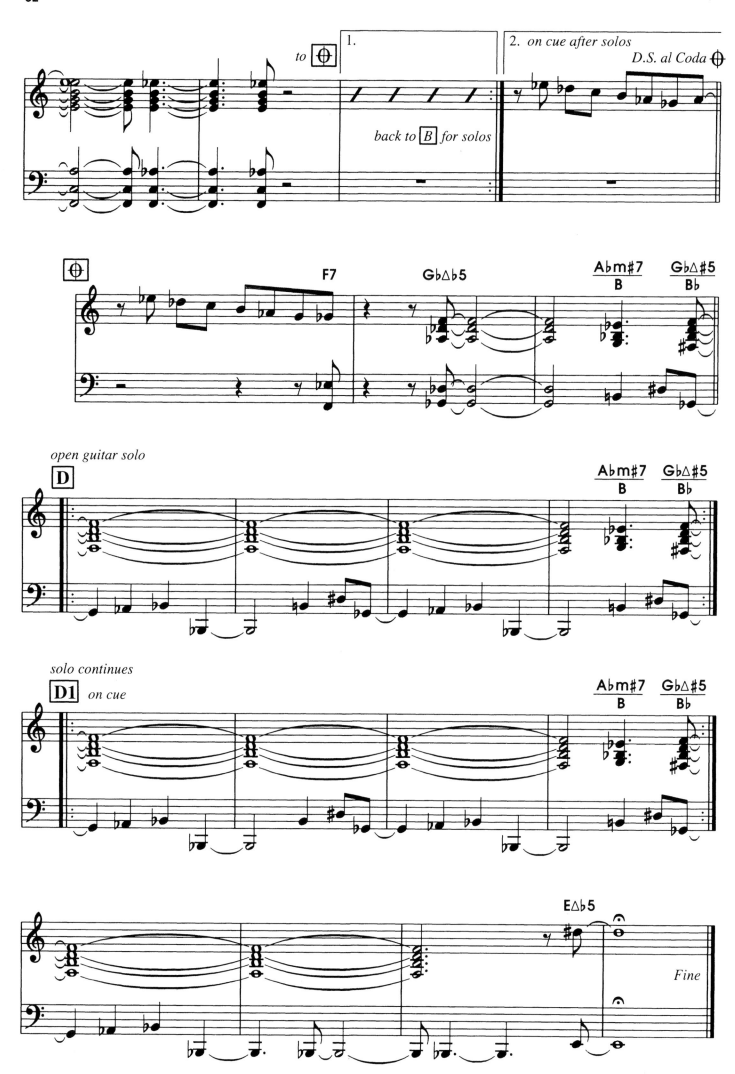

ISHED

By CHICK COREA
and JIMMY EARL

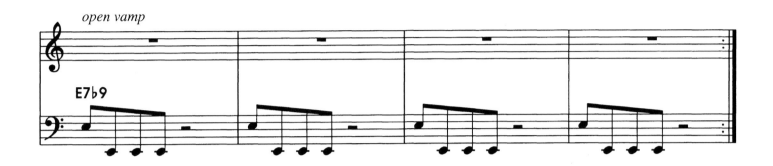

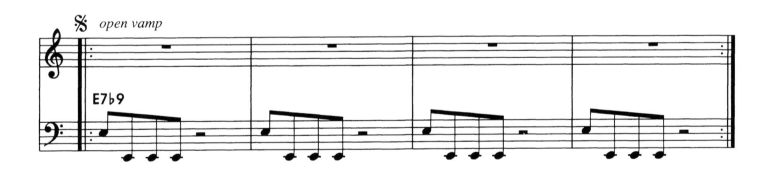

SPANISH SKETCH

By CHICK COREA

B "flamenco" Basic Scale

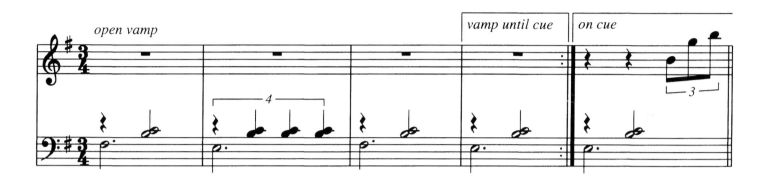

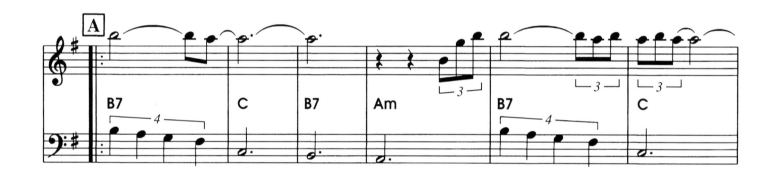

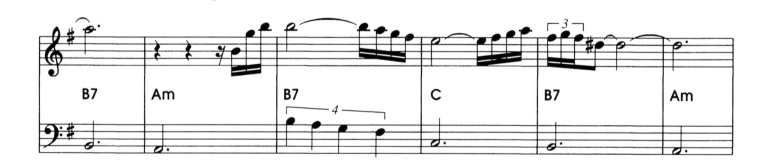

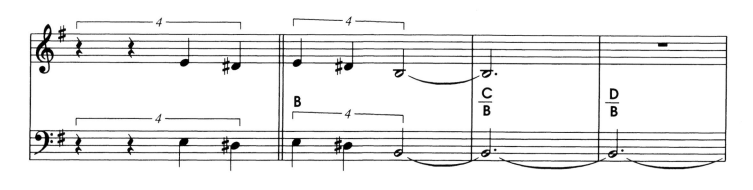

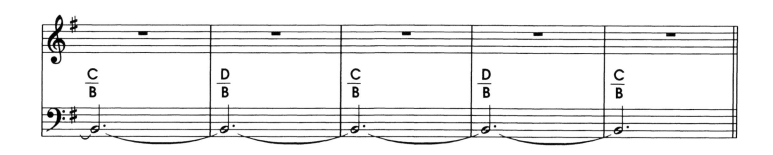

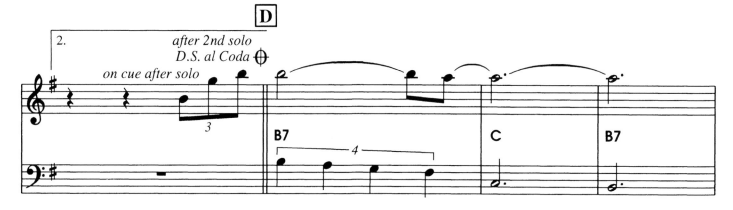

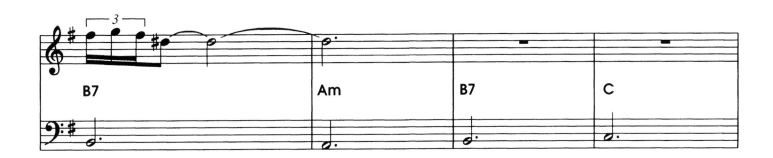

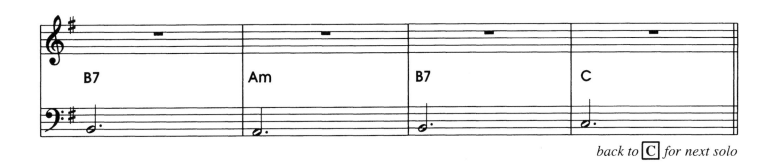

back to C *for next solo*

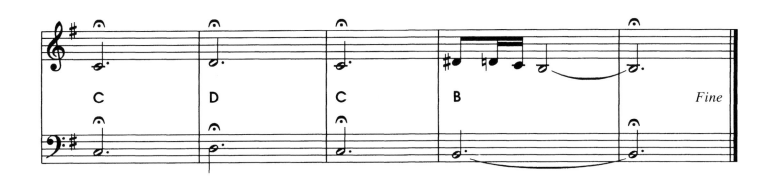

ARTIST TRANSCRIPTIONS®

Artist Transcriptions are authentic, note-for-note transcriptions of today's hottest artists in jazz, pop and rock. These outstanding, accurate arrangements are in an easy-to-read format which includes all essential lines. **Artist Transcriptions** can be used to perform, sequence or for reference.

FLUTE

00672379	Eric Dolphy Collection	$19.95
00672582	The Very Best of James Galway	$19.99
00672372	James Moody Collection – Sax and Flute	$19.95

GUITAR & BASS

00660113	Guitar Style of George Benson	$19.99
00672573	Ray Brown – Legendary Jazz Bassist	$22.99
00672331	Ron Carter Collection	$24.99
00660115	Al Di Meola – Friday Night in San Francisco	$24.99
00125617	Best of Herb Ellis	$19.99
00699306	Jim Hall – Exploring Jazz Guitar	$19.99
00672353	The Joe Pass Collection	$22.99
00673216	John Patitucci	$22.99
00672374	Johnny Smith – Guitar Solos	$24.99

PIANO & KEYBOARD

00672487	Monty Alexander Plays Standards	$19.95
00672520	Count Basie Collection	$19.95
00192307	Bebop Piano Legends	$19.99
00113680	Blues Piano Legends	$22.99
00672526	The Bill Charlap Collection	$19.99
00278003	A Charlie Brown Christmas	$19.99
00672300	Chick Corea – Paint the World	$19.99
00146105	Bill Evans – Alone	$21.99
00672548	The Mastery of Bill Evans	$16.99
00672365	Bill Evans – Play Standards	$22.99
00121885	Bill Evans – Time Remembered	$22.99
00672510	Bill Evans Trio Vol. 1: 1959-1961	$29.99
00672511	Bill Evans Trio Vol. 2: 1962-1965	$27.99
00672512	Bill Evans Trio Vol. 3: 1968-1974	$29.99
00672513	Bill Evans Trio Vol. 4: 1979-1980	$24.95
00193332	Erroll Garner – Concert by the Sea	$22.99
00672486	Vince Guaraldi Collection	$19.99
00289644	The Definitive Vince Guaraldi	$39.99
00672419	Herbie Hancock Collection	$22.99
00672438	Hampton Hawes Collection	$19.95
00672322	Ahmad Jamal Collection	$27.99
00255671	Jazz Piano Masterpieces	$22.99
00124367	Jazz Piano Masters Play Rodgers & Hammerstein	$19.99
00672564	Best of Jeff Lorber	$19.99

00672476	Brad Mehldau Collection	$24.99
00672388	Best of Thelonious Monk	$22.99
00672389	Thelonious Monk Collection	$24.99
00672390	Thelonious Monk Plays Jazz Standards – Volume 1	$24.99
00672391	Thelonious Monk Plays Jazz Standards – Volume 2	$24.99
00672433	Jelly Roll Morton – The Piano Rolls	$19.99
00264094	Oscar Peterson – Night Train	$19.99
00672544	Oscar Peterson – Originals	$15.99
00672531	Oscar Peterson – Plays Duke Ellington	$27.99
00672563	Oscar Peterson – A Royal Wedding Suite	$19.99
00672569	Oscar Peterson – Tracks	$19.99
00672533	Oscar Peterson – Trios	$39.99
00672534	Very Best of Oscar Peterson	$27.99
00672371	Bud Powell Classics	$22.99
00672376	Bud Powell Collection	$24.99
00672507	Gonzalo Rubalcaba Collection	$19.95
00672303	Horace Silver Collection	$24.99
00672316	Art Tatum Collection	$27.99
00672355	Art Tatum Solo Book	$22.99
00672357	The Billy Taylor Collection	$24.95
00673215	McCoy Tyner	$22.99
00672321	Cedar Walton Collection	$19.95
00672519	Kenny Werner Collection	$19.95

SAXOPHONE

00672566	The Mindi Abair Collection	$14.99
00673244	Julian "Cannonball" Adderley Collection	$22.99
00673237	Michael Brecker	$24.99
00672429	Michael Brecker Collection	$24.99
00672529	John Coltrane – Giant Steps	$22.99
00672494	John Coltrane – A Love Supreme	$17.99
00672493	John Coltrane Plays "Coltrane Changes"	$19.95
00672453	John Coltrane Plays Standards	$24.99
00673233	John Coltrane Solos	$29.99
00672328	Paul Desmond Collection	$22.99
00672530	Kenny Garrett Collection	$24.99
00699375	Stan Getz	$19.99
00672377	Stan Getz – Bossa Novas	$24.99
00673254	Great Tenor Sax Solos	$22.99

00672523	Coleman Hawkins Collection	$24.99
00672330	Best of Joe Henderson	$24.99
00673239	Best of Kenny G	$22.99
00673229	Kenny G – Breathless	$19.99
00672462	Kenny G – Classics in the Key of G	$24.99
00672485	Kenny G – Faith: A Holiday Album	$17.99
00672373	Kenny G – The Moment	$22.99
00672498	Jackie McLean Collection	$19.95
00672372	James Moody Collection – Sax and Flute	$19.95
00672539	Gerry Mulligan Collection	$24.99
00102751	Sonny Rollins, Art Blakey & Kenny Drew with the Modern Jazz Quartet	$17.99
00675000	David Sanborn Collection	$19.99
00672491	The New Best of Wayne Shorter	$24.99
00672550	The Sonny Stitt Collection	$19.95
00672524	Lester Young Collection	$22.99

TROMBONE

00672332	J.J. Johnson Collection	$24.99
00672489	Steve Turré Collection	$19.99

TRUMPET

00672557	Herb Alpert Collection	$19.99
00672480	Louis Armstrong Collection	$19.99
00672481	Louis Armstrong Plays Standards	$19.99
00672435	Chet Baker Collection	$24.99
00672556	Best of Chris Botti	$19.99
00672448	Miles Davis – Originals, Vol. 1	$19.99
00672451	Miles Davis – Originals, Vol. 2	$19.99
00672449	Miles Davis – Standards, Vol. 2	$19.95
00672479	Dizzy Gillespie Collection	$19.95
00673214	Freddie Hubbard	$19.99
00672506	Chuck Mangione Collection	$22.99
00672525	Arturo Sandoval – Trumpet Evolution	$19.99

HAL•LEONARD®

Visit our web site for songlists or to order online from your favorite music retailer at
www.halleonard.com